KINGFISHER READERS

level 1

Butterflies

Thea Feldman

KINGFISHER

KINGFISHER

First published 2012 by Kingfisher
an imprint of Macmillan Children's Books
a division of Macmillan Publishers Limited
20 New Wharf Road, London N1 9RR
Basingstoke and Oxford
Associated companies throughout the world
www.panmacmillan.com

Series editor: Heather Morris
Literacy consultant: Hilary Horton

ISBN: 978-0-7534-3314-0
Copyright © Macmillan Publishers Ltd 2012

9 8 7 6 5 4 3 2 1

1TR/1011/WKT/UNTD/105MA

A CIP catalogue record for this book is available from the British Library.

Printed in China

Picture credits
The Publisher would like to thank the following for permission to reproduce their material. Every care has been taken
to trace copyright holders. However, if there have been unintentional omissions or failure to trace copyright holders, we
apologize and will, if informed, endeavour to make corrections in any future edition.
Top = t; Bottom = b; Centre = c; Left = l; Right = r
Cover Shutterstock/Kuttelvaserova; Pages 3 Photolibrary/Bios; 3 Shutterstock/Serg64; 4 Photoshot/NHPA/Jordi
Bas Casas; 5 Corbis/Papillo; 6t Photolibrary/Bios; 6b Shutterstock/nodiff; 7cl Frank Lane Picture Agency (FLPA)/
Wim Reyns/Minden; 7cr Shutterstock/freepainter; 7bl Photolibrary/Superstock; 7br Corbis/Tim Zurowski/All
Canada Photos; 8 Photolibrary/Bios; 9 Shutterstock/SaraJo; 10t Shutterstock/Miles Boyar; 10b Corbis/Darrell
Gulin; 11t Shutterstock/Willem Dijkstra; 11b FLPA/Malcolm Schuyl; 12 Getty/flickr; 13 Photoshot/NHPA/ Jordi Bas
Casas; 14 Alamy/Natural History Museum; 15 Alamy/Corbis; 16 Getty/Darrell Gulin; 17 Photolibrary/Imagebroker;
18–19 FLPA/Michael Weber; 19 Shutterstock/Olga Bogatyrenko; 20 Naturepl/Ingo Arndt; 21 Photoshot/NHPA/
T. Hitchin & V. Hurst; 22 Photolibrary/OSF; 23 Photolibrary/Animals Animals; 24t FLPA/WaterFrame; 24b Alamy/
Don Johnston; 25t Naturepl/Doug Wechsler; 25b Photolibrary/Peter Arnold Images; 26l Photolibrary/Don
Johnston; 26r Alamy/Phil Degginger; 27 Corbis/Skip Moody/Rainbow; 28 Naturepl/Ingo Arndt; 29 Corbis/
T. Hitchin & V. Hurst; 30–31 Getty/Iconica; 30–31 Naturepl/Stephen Dalton.

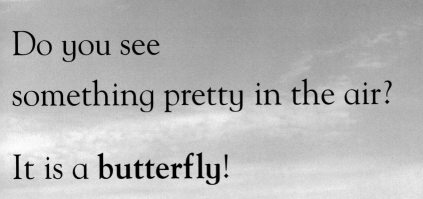

Do you see
something pretty in the air?

It is a **butterfly**!

A butterfly is an **insect**.

Not all insects can fly.

But butterflies do!

Butterflies have wings.

The wings are covered
in tiny scales.

Some butterflies are colourful.

Look at these colourful butterflies!

Birds, snakes and other animals eat butterflies.

But colourful butterflies can stay safe.

A colourful butterfly may taste bad.

It may have poison in its body.

Its colours warn other animals not to eat it.

How else do butterflies
stay safe?

Some butterflies have big spots
on their wings.

The spots look like big, scary eyes.

The spots keep hungry animals away.

This is a **moth**.

Moths and butterflies
look like each other.

But they are different.

One way they are different
is that moths fly at night.

Butterflies fly in the daytime.

This is the biggest butterfly.
It is bigger than this book.

This is the
smallest butterfly.
This picture
shows it life size.

Butterflies look for flowers.

They drink **nectar** from flowers.

Slurp!

A butterfly's tongue is like
a drinking straw.

How can a butterfly tell
if a flower tastes good?

It uses its feet.

A butterfly's **taste buds** are on its feet.

Where are your taste buds?

A butterfly lays eggs on leaves.

The eggs will hatch
by themselves.

Surprise!

Look who comes out.
A **caterpillar**.

A caterpillar does not
look like a butterfly.

But a caterpillar is
a baby butterfly.

Munch, munch, munch.

The caterpillar eats and eats.

It eats leaves.

The caterpillar grows and grows.

One day the caterpillar
stops eating.

It makes a safe place to stay.

The safe place is called
a **chrysalis**.

It stays inside the chrysalis
for a few weeks.

Surprise!

Look who comes out.

The caterpillar
is now a butterfly.

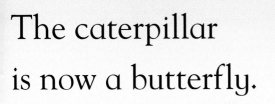

Do you see something pretty
in the air?

It is a butterfly, all grown up!

Glossary

butterfly a type of insect that flies in the daytime

caterpillar a baby butterfly

chrysalis a place a caterpillar makes that keeps it safe for a few weeks while it turns into a butterfly

insect a type of small animal with six legs

moth a type of insect that flies at night

nectar a sweet juice found in flowers that butterflies drink with their tongues

taste buds tiny parts of the body that can tell what something tastes like. People have taste buds on the tongue. Butterflies have taste buds on the feet.